Trauma Queen

EmilyAnn Howe

Presentation by *BookLeaf Publishing*

Web: www.bookleafpub.com

E-mail: info@bookleafpub.com

ISBN: 9789357744140

First edition 2023

To my children- Bug, Luu, Pay, Tee, Kate, E, & Li, and the power of healing generational trauma. My greatest joy in life is being your mom.

To Shannon Kellie- I found my best friend for life and soulmate at 15. Thank you for loving me through it all and having my back when I needed it.

To David- the very first man who said I love you and meant it. I love you more than anything.

ACKNOWLEDGEMENT

I'd like to thank Mrs. Tammy and the staff of The Village (Robeson Healthcare) in Winterville NC. I would not be here today without you. Mrs. Leticia, I remember when you said I had a book hidden in me. That moment has stayed with me and pushed me to finish this project.

PREFACE

A warning to the reader that the subject material contained herein is at times difficult and triggering to read. I struggled with this project at times and didn't think I'd see it through. There's a hope that sharing my reflections will help to ease someone else's pain. My biggest takeaway from rehab was that secrets keep you sick. I've found this to be true. In that light, this book has been a catharsis of sorts for me. I hope you enjoy it.

If you or someone you love is struggling with mental health or substance abuse issues you can find help at www.samhsa.gov

Writer's Block

I know the story, it's mine to tell.
Putting words on paper always fails.
After surviving years of abuse and pain,
I wonder what the trauma did to my brain.
I was a gifted child, could read by three.
So what the hell is wrong with me?
Dreams of being an author, a longing to write,
Just putting pen to paper, bringing the story to
life.
Ideas, ponderings, things to say...
When I try to write, it fades away.
My vocabulary seems nowhere in sight.
The page stares at me, blank and white.

Anxiety

It's not til the pressure burns in her chest,
She even realizes she's holding her breath.
She's safe now, this she knows.
Yet her body is tense, awaiting the blows.
She can't remember the last time she slept,
Without waking up covered in sweat.
She's learned the alchemy of turning fear to rage.
Still, she guards her triggers with a cage.

When I Was Two

I saw my father for the last time, he took me to
the zoo.
Then Mommy married a new man, and we
moved.
I got ten stitches after a lost sword fight.
How'd my four-year-old brother get a real knife?
There were Flinstone's baby bottles
and Wonder Woman Underoos.
A doll named Honey,
And a kitchen set too.
Playdates with Heather,
Climbing the apple tree,
And when the chicken pox
Got my brothers and me.
Maw-maw and Paw-paw
Right up the street.
On Sundays,
We went there to eat.
Begging my grandparents
To spend the night.
Crying for my dad
When they shut off the lights.
Frilly dresses that twirled,
With lace and bows...
And black patent leather shoes

With fancy toes.
Happy childhood memories,
There are so few.
The trauma hadn't started yet,
not when I was two.

Good Girl

Be a good girl,
Follow the rules.
Memorize your verses
For Sunday school.
Sit up! Don't slouch in the pew.
Sing whatever solo
Pastor asks of you.

Be a good girl,
Do well in class.
Listen to teacher,
And don't you dare sass.
You're such a smart girl,
Look at those A's!
And we'll beat you
For any other grade.

Be a good girl,
Finish your chores,
You know what happens if not,
When I come through the door.

Be a good girl,
Take a bath,
Brush your teeth,

Then come to my room
When your sisters are asleep.

Be a good girl,
You must never tell Mommy,
Dad's gonna teach you a game.
And if you tell her,
You'll take the blame.

Now be a good girl,
Just open your mouth
And I'll guide your head,
Then we'll take off your undies,
And climb in my bed.

Be a good girl,
Open your legs real wide.
For now, you're too small,
I'll just have to grind.

You're not a good girl.
And it's all your fault,
You told Mommy
And now I'm caught.

You're not a good girl,
And you'd better not tell,
Or we'll call you a liar
And put you in juvenile jail.

You're not a good girl,
That's why you're hit.
You told on Daddy,
And he doesn't like it
Not one bit.

You're not a good girl,
But if you know
What's best for you,
You'll keep your mouth shut
About the abuse.

So, be a good girl,
Yes, that's it!
The picture of poise,
Grace, and wit.

Be a good girl,
Keep up those grades
And never EVER tell them
How you were raised.

Running Away

I didn't get very far the first time I ran away,
Before my neighbor sent my mother my way.
I always knew I didn't belong.
My family lived there, but it wasn't a home.
There were three bedrooms, a mom and a dad.
A brother, a sister, a dog and some cats.
A house of horrors, with roaches and mice,
That crawled in your bed, ran all over at night.
A place with rules subject to change.
And the slightest misstep was sure to cause pain,
I remember the sting of the buckle across my
face.
Some kids had parents, I had monsters in their
place.

The second time I ran, I left with a friend.
My fear, alone in the woods, took me home
again.
Hauled to the station, what could I say,
When the police asked me why I ran that day?
I remember threatening to reveal the abuse.
I was so small, broken and bruised.
I knew better than to breathe a word
Or even hint at the abuse I'd endured.
So I made up a story, crazy and wild,

Let them label me the problem child.
I went back to that house, to the monsters at
home.
And there I stayed put until I was grown.

I no longer lived there, hadn't in a while,
But the last time I left, I went 800 miles.
Boarding the bus, alone and bereft,
Holding the pieces of me that were left.
I went for long walks, and talked to the trees,
And little by little, finally found peace.

Hey, Mr. RIpley

Hey Mr. Ripley, spare a second for me.
I've got a story even you wouldn't believe.
It starts on a Wednesday, a cold winter morning,
And the birth of a daughter nobody wanted.
They say Wednesday's child is full of woe.
That's exactly how this story goes.
The third child, and illegitimate daughter.
Given another man's name, not her father's.
Maybe it's better he kept his name after all.
He was gone by two, no letters, no call.
They went to the zoo on their very last day.
Then he moved three states away.
Her mother remarried before she was three,
And her new dad ruled with tyranny.
He kicked her once across the room,
For not cleaning, too small for the broom.
There was a chill that ran down her spine
When Momma threatened Daddy would be
home at five.
These words no idle threat.
Still surprised he didn't beat her to death.
And so, she learned to follow the rules.
To sit still in church and do well in school.
She learned to keep quiet, their secrets
concealed.

And covered the bruises with sleeves til they
healed.
She remembers when they had no power,
Going to her grandma's for meals and showers.
By this time his girls were born.
They were the roses, she a thorn.
She dreamed of her dad showing up one day,
Picking her up, taking her away.
The years went by and he never came.
So the new Daddy taught her a game.
These horrors continued to sixth grade,
When she could no longer take it and blurted it
out one day.
She thought that would be the end of the pain,
Surely her mother would end his reign.
But the monster returned that very night,
and continued to fill her with fright.
Then one day the monster was dead,
And her mother refused to get out of bed.
And so, she gained the kids and house.
Then drank on the weekends to let it all out.
Add to the mix a bipolar brother.
With a tendency to harm himself and others.
She learned to fight, punch and kick.
Had no choice, she was his favorite pick.
He was a mad man free of his cage.
And she the target of his rage.
When she appealed for help, her Momma would
say,

What did you do to make him act this way?
Desperate to leave there'd be an engagement,
Before her graduation.
But wedding bells were put on hold
After a night with a waitress when the groom's
feet got cold.
When it was over to ease her pain,
She hit up an old friend and went to his game.
There was a big party for the season win,
And the next morning she woke up with him.
She'd know she was pregnant in a few weeks.
But she wasn't the only girl, there were three.
She reconciled with her ex, gave bio dad the
option,
He couldn't agree fast enough to the adoption.
And so she celebrated the birth of her son,
And was expecting his sister before he was one.
Before the birth of baby two, early one morning,
Her marriage ended with no warning.
She knows that letter saved her life.
Because the author met her demise at the end of
his knife.
She found herself charged with the burden
Of telling her kids Daddy had murdered.
And how do you tell a child of three and one of
five
That Daddy's the reason his girlfriend died?
When the trial was over, he went to prison.
They slowly rebuilt their lives, bit by bit.

But then her daughter was attacked by a
neighbor's son.
For the first time she considered murder, loaded
the gun.
She thought to herself "my God, it's finally
happened,
They finally pushed me too far, I'm actually
snapping."
Then she thought of her son and daughter,
Already growing up without their father.
She let out a primal scream and a gut-wrenching
sob,
Then let the justice system do its job.
And early one morning much to her fright,
While driving to work, she lost her sight.
There were tests, surgeries, and hospital beds,
And a shunt to drain the fluid from her head.
What came next was cocaine addiction.
And fucking up life beyond recognition.
A criminal record and ruined reputation.
Ending with a stay in drug rehabilitation.
She lost her car, house, and kids,
Then found herself back on drugs again.
She didn't care if she lived or died,
Couldn't think of a reason to be alive.
But in all that darkness, devoid of light,
A voice said to her "Girl, get up and fight".
She packed up her bags and went far away.
Little by little she healed each day.

In the end you'll find her happy and thriving.
Living her best life, no longer just surviving.
What's that Mr. Ripley? How do I know it's true?
Well, because I survived to tell it to you.

My Mother

I became a mother, and finally understood,
You never actually loved me and never would.
You gave me shelter, but never a home.
In a house of seven, I was alone.
You put clothes on my back and shoes on my
feet.
Then sat there silently while my brother and I
got beat.
You took us to church, made us pray.
Then took us home to be your slaves.
Always quick to remind us, lest we complain,
That the reason you had kids was to have maids.
We lost power because you failed to pay bills.
You sent us on to school even when we were ill.
You taught us to lie and deny the truth.
To say we were fine and hide the abuse.
Somehow I thought you were my friend.
But you were only less evil than him.

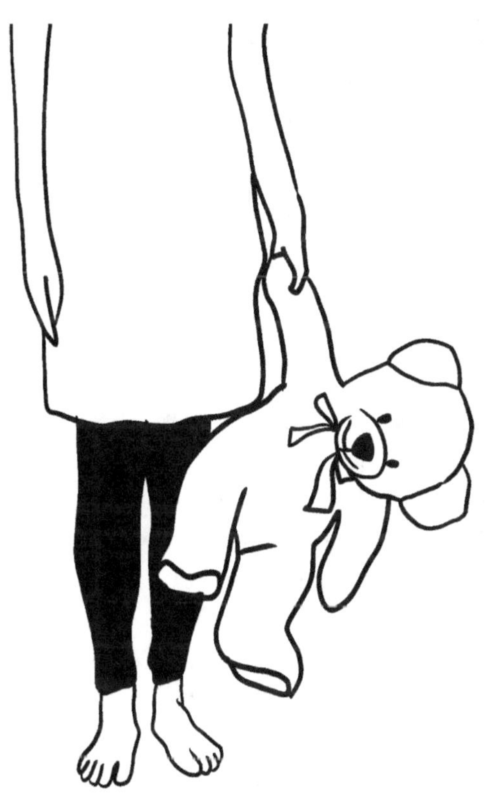

Mommy Dearest

You can't believe I did drugs.
You damn sure didn't raise me that way.
That's so freaking funny, Momma.
And exactly what I knew you'd say.
How'd I end up an addict?
Hmmm... let's see.
We'll explore it together, Momma
Just you and me.
I'm no black sheep,
Bitch, those are bruises.
From years at the hands
Of unspeakable abuses.
Go on, Momma, deny the truth.
That the passing of trauma
Down through generations
is directly responsible
For my self-medication.
I'm no longer keeping secrets,
I decided to tell.
And I don't care that you're offended
I told you to rot in hell.
I'm in my forties,
My vision the clearest,
I no longer need you,
Mommy Dearest.

Trauma Manifested

It's interesting to see how trauma plays out,
Amongst different kids from the same house.
One son got married and never looked back,
Embarrassed by what his family lacked.
The other son couldn't get it together if he tried,
In and out of jail, stealing folks' wives.
A daughter was next, child number three.
She coped with alcohol, drugs, and life in the
streets.
Daughter number four in the fold,
Grew angry and hostile, bitter and cold.
The youngest daughter, sweet baby girl,
Lives entirely in her own false world.
A couple are working in an effort to heal.
The others don't see a problem and never will.

For April

The ghost of a girl
I met once in life,
And once in a dream,
Stares back at me
From the TV screen.
Then there's the ghost
Of the girl I used to be.
The two of us, linked forever
By falling in love with a monster
Neither of us could see.
Wisdom is wasted on the youth
That's what the old folks say,
But damned if I don't wish
I'd had some in those days.
But I was so naive and young,
And already traumatized by
The monster at home.
And this boy was different
From everyone I'd known.
There were poems and flowers,
Long romantic, elaborate letters
That had to take hours.
And before I knew it
I was swept off my feet.
How the hell was I to know

What love bombing was at fourteen?
I fell for the whole chivalrous bit,
The hint of danger,
The wounded kid.
We married after high school
Had a son
Then pregnant with a daughter,
I left before she was born.
She soon took my place in his life
Played her part, hated me,
Believed his lies.
He abandoned his children
Barely paid his support,
Then played the victim
When drug into court.
And shortly after his daughter was one,
Her new half-sister was born.
They signed the papers,
Gave up their rights,
And three months later
Came the violent fights.
She left him behind
And went to her mom's.
But the separation only lasted
a short few months.
She came back,
They rekindled the flame.
He promised to divorce me,
And give her his name.

Then, a year or so later,
Pregnant with her daughter,
They both lost their lives
At the hands of the child's father.

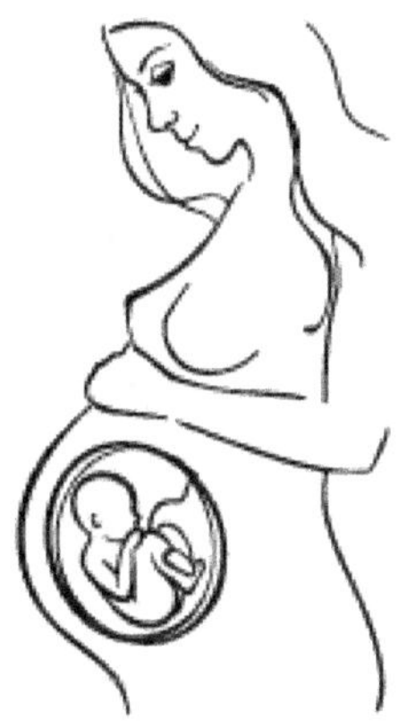

Love and War

I never understood the Romans and Greek.
How was one goddess of both love and war?
I'm older now and life made me hard.
I left behind all I ever knew,
Threw a match to their lies and took my truth.
Not a care for what they thought,
My freedom was hard won, hard fought.
The luxury of trust I can no longer afford.
I don't get attached and keep one foot out the
door.
Love is a word used only to trick.
So know if you say it, I'm outta here, quick.

Just Ask Roe

Asherah's angry, do you hear her call?
Sisters, listen. She speaks to us all.
They murdered Yahweh's wife, erased her from
the pages.
Then passed their masochism down through the
ages.
They robbed Mother God of her rights,
Based her value on her performance as a wife.
They banned her from speaking in the church,
Took away her voice.
Then they took possession of her body and gave
her no choice.
They denied her land, freedom, wealth.
Made her dependent on someone else.
And when Lillith refused, they banned her from
Paradise,
And set about making Adam's new wife.
Eve was created from his rib,
Her sole purpose to serve him.
They put her in charge of the house and the kids.
Took all of her power, gave it to men.
And spoke of damnation and fire,
For refusing her husband's desires.
But women have rights now, doncha know?
Sure we do, Just ask Roe.

To Be American

A nation divided, everyone at odds.
That's how they like it to keep their jobs.
They feed us opinions disguised as the truth.
And lie to us daily on the six o'clock news.
They've divided us with religion and race,
And watch as chaos engulfs the place.
The ads are the same every four years.
Votes are cast off baseless fears.
They tell us their lies, give us false hope,
And disappear to Washington once they get the
vote.
So, life goes on stuck in this cage.
Violence erupts from long suppressed rage.
We take to the streets to protest and march,
And if that doesn't work, we light up the torch.
Breaking the windows, burning the place down.
Leave nothing of value in our own hometowns.
It happens so often, we're barely stunned,
When a kid shows up at school and unloads his
gun.
We lie to the youth and crush their dreams.
And push them out of school before they can
even read.
We're a culture obsessed with money and power,
We'll sacrifice our family to work more hours.

No one is happy, depression makes millions.
And if you can't focus, we'll give you stimulants.
If you don't have healthcare, you can't afford this
shit.
No worries, just visit your local street
pharmacist.
Nothing will change no matter how hard we try,
Until we recognize the problem is not you or I.
Every person who was born on this land
Is the same as you, an American.
So when you stand up for the rights promised to
you,
Don't forget to stand for theirs too.

All Hell; The Queen

You see the crown, the pretty jewels.
You see the clothes, cars, bags and shoes.
You see the pictures from the vacations.
You've lost track of the trips she's taken.
Don't be fooled by the mirrors and smoke.
There's a side to the crown so few know.
The money is a gilded trap.
It can buy everything but the attention she lacks.
It may look like a fairy tale to all who see.
But the weight of the crown is heavy in the seat.
The wife of the king? She's no reason to
complain.
Couldn't possibly be lonely or in any pain.
There was a time before all the glitz,
When money was tight, but love was bliss.
You see the king, she sees a ghost.
And when he's at home, she misses him most.
He wanted his riches without all the hassle,
So he bought her a shiny new castle.
Now he's in the castle only to eat,
Complain, make demands, and sleep.
But to say this out loud is treason to the king.
So, the Queen smiles and dies in her seat.

When You're Gone

You're hardly here,
and when you're home,
You can't be bothered
to put down your phone.
You throw tantrums
to get your way.
You are often ruthless
with the words you say.
To tell the truth,
I like being alone.
It's so much more peaceful
When you're gone.

Self-Medication

I went to drug rehabilitation
to put an end to self-medication.
I passed my screens, went to the group,
but carefully guarded my painful truth.
Picked up some skills meant to help cope.
Learned a few mantras, nourished some hope.
But if nothing changes, nothing changes.
And the streets are still there with all their
dangers.
So, I finally made myself do the work,
Dealt with my trauma, cleaned up my dirt.
Got honest with myself and apologized to
friends,
And did my best to make amends.
I'm still angry and struggle to forgive.
But I've rediscovered my will to live.
Healing the hurt before the next generation
Ends up trying self-medication.

ADHD

It's always running incredibly late.
It's absolutely nothing or too much to say.
It's forgetting to text or call.
Forgetting where my car is at the mall.
It's zoning out, thoughts drifting away.
And having to ask "what did you say?"
It's struggling to hear my husband's voice
Because there's too much background noise.
It's starting the laundry, then the dishes.
Then cleaning my room before either is finished.
It's never being ready to leave home
Because I've lost my keys or phone.
It's struggling with a high IQ
And a list of things I'll never do.
It's clutter on dresser tops,
And baskets of unmatched socks.
It's going days without a shower,
Being wide awake at the midnight hour.
An intense hatred of mundane tasks,
And a loss of focus in class.
It's related conditions, dyspraxia and depression,
Anxiety disorders and the Autism Spectrum.
It's understanding that hyperactivity means
Trying at once, to do all of the things.
it's every few weeks a brand new passion

About which I incessantly babble.
It's living a life of constant extremes,
All the while mining for dopamine.

Music Heals

I may struggle with what to say,
but the lyrics find a way.
The music absorbs the pain
and I'm myself again.
There's a song for any mood.
I can dance, I can brood.
Reggae, Hip-hop, Rock, Country, Blues
And don't you dare step on Elvis' shoes.
Foghat took us on a slow ride.
Elton taught us the meaning of PRIDE.
Slash shredded that fucking guitar,
Zepplin took us on a stairway to the stars.
In Mercury, we found our Queen.
And Strait ol' George is Country's King.
Music brings the party to life,
Takes us back, sets the vibe.
It's the one universal tool
With the power to unite me and you.

These Days

A mobile home on a city lot.
A medical card and top shelf pot.
My grandson's laugh and precious smile.
His Momma's house down the road a quarter
mile.
Two grown sons, night and day.
Wonder who baby boy will be someday.
A Pisces daughter after my heart,
Our birthdays a week apart.
A bonus daughter with a military man,
A prayer he's not sent to a foreign land.
The youngest daughter eight years old,
The comeback? Greatest ever told.

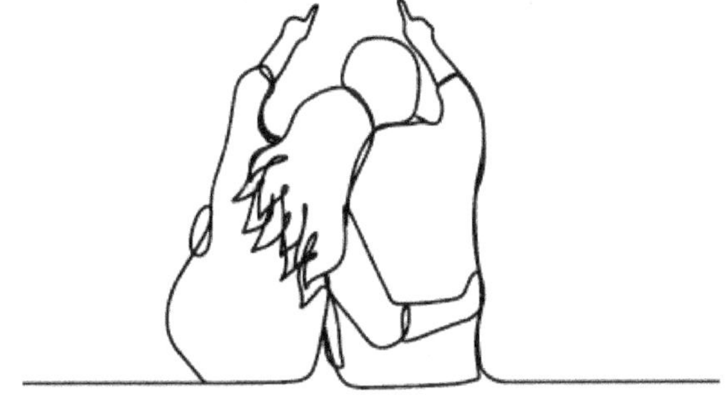

David

I packed up my trauma, you brought your own.
Together we set out to build our home.
You had your ways, I had mine.
It caused disagreement time after time.
There were years we barely made it,
Everything tense, every word hateful.
You blamed me, I blamed you.
And we stayed tangled in a web of abuse.
Tired of fighting, we took off our gloves,
Everything shattered, but still there was love.
We moved away, left it behind.
Listened for once, learned to be kind.
For better or worse we tested each vow.
And miraculously never threw in the towel.
Now we watch our grandboys grow.
They said we wouldn't make it. What'd they
know?

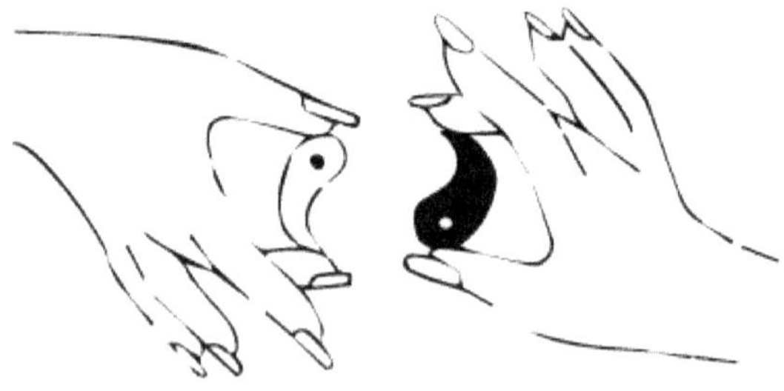

The Trees

I climbed their branches,
Cooled off in their shade.
They held up my tree house,
Under the canopy, I played.
And when the world
Is too much for me,
I return home,
To the trees.